Love, Grace, Mercy & Favor (Know the Differences and Uses)

Joshua Olumoye

Published by Joshua Olumoye, 2023.

SKU: 0025

Cover design by: JOO

Email: harmonyheavenlychurch@gmail.com

Phone: +1 7344474400

Printed in the United States of America

Table of Contents

ACKNOWLEDGEMENTS

I hereby use this page to acknowledge all the people whom God have use to prepare me for the ministry.

I acknowledge all the men of God whom God uses to pray for me day and night, I pray your labor of love will never be in vain. Also, I thank my family and loved one for their prayer and support.

Finally, I acknowledge the God Almighty whom through the Holy Spirit keep and guide me into all things.

DEDICATION

This book is dedicated to God the Father, God the Son, and God the Holy Spirit.

INTRODUCTION

LOVE, GRACE, MERCY, AND FAVOR

Ephesians 2:4-5

4 But God, who is rich in mercy, for his great love wherewith he loved us,

5 Even when we were dead in sins, hath quickened us together with Christ, (by grace ye are saved;)

Love, grace, mercy, and favor are four major characteristics of God that we cannot do without, and these characteristics are all related to one another, so if you have one of them you are likely to have the other. But in all it is better to have all of them.

This book will explain the different between these characters of God, how to get them, how to keep them and how to restore them when they are lost.

Love is God and God is love. God is not just loving but God is love himself.

1 John 4:7-8

7 Beloved, let us love one another: for love is of God; and every one that loveth is born of God, and knoweth God.

8 He that loveth not knoweth not God; for God is love.

The word love in real essence is God, God love is not about believers alone but for the whole world.

John 3:16

16 For God so loved the world, that he gave his only begotten Son, that whosoever believeth in him should not perish, but have everlasting life.

The love of God is extended to the whole world, but the eternal life is extended through his son to those who believe in the son only.

But the good news is that the eternal life is available at any point you believe in the son, but the bad news is you might not have time to believe if you do not believe now.

Yeshua is for whosoever will believe Jews or Gentiles.

Grace is another characteristic of God that is similar but manifested after the falling of men at this time men have fell out of love with God, but God need to keep human race alive, and grace of God choose Noah not because he is qualified but because he is not qualified but for grace.

Genesis 6:1-8

1 And it came to pass, when men began to multiply on the face of the earth, and daughters were born unto them,

2 That the sons of God saw the daughters of men that they were fair; and they took them wives of all which they chose.

3 And the Lord said, My spirit shall not always strive with man, for that he also is flesh: yet his days shall be an hundred and twenty years.

4 There were giants in the earth in those days; and also after that, when the sons of God came in unto the daughters of men, and they bare children to them, the same became mighty men which were of old, men of renown.

5 And God saw that the wickedness of man was great in the earth, and that every imagination of the thoughts of his heart was only evil continually.

6 And it repented the Lord that he had made man on the earth, and it grieved him at his heart.

7 And the Lord said, I will destroy man whom I have created from the face of the earth; both man, and beast, and the creeping thing, and the fowls of the air; for it repenteth me that I have made them.

8 But Noah found grace in the eyes of the Lord.

That is why grace is defined as unmerited favor, that is the extension of love to someone who deserve no love.

You need nothing to qualify you for grace for it is a gift of God.

Mercy of God is a product of love and grace of God, mercy came after God revealed himself to mankind, to the Israelites and men still refuses to acknowledge God but want to continue in their sinful state and for God not to wipe out the human race again mercy speak.

Mercy is the blood of Yeshua which became the platform through which God can relate to men.

It is of the Lord mercy we are not consumed by God or by the enemies.

Lamentations 3:22

22 It is of the Lord's mercies that we are not consumed, because his compassions fail not.

Mercy deals solely with judgement and justice while we were still alive, and it is always victorious over judgement. Mercy does not work after we die.

James 2:13

13 For he shall have judgment without mercy, that hath shewed no mercy; and mercy rejoiceth against judgment.

Mercy is not automatic; you need repentance to qualify for mercy and effective prayers to obtain mercy.

Favor is that part of God that deals with preference and choice, in this case God has favorite among his loved children, that is God preferred you to another.

Favor makes you best among equal.

Psalm 45:7

7 Thou lovest righteousness, and hatest wickedness: therefore God, thy God, hath anointed thee with the oil of gladness above thy fellows.

Favor is complicated than we thought, because we often believed that those who are not favored are hated by God, but it is not so, but it is just that those whom God favored are preferred above others.

For example, bible says Mary is highly favored among virgins, and in this case, God can only choose one virgin and Mary is chosen, what about Esau and Jacob God choses Jacob

And it is often replaced by love, grace, or mercy, for in the case of Esau and Jacob it is favor and not just love and hate.

You need to be in alignment with God to qualify for his favor.

These four special characteristics of God are indeed special, they all speak and act.

Love gives his all and he never fail, Grace speaks unstoppable and preservation, Mercy speaks justification in judgement, favor choses you when others rejected you.

And in all we need at least one of these characteristics of God and others will come.

CHAPTER 1

LOVE

WHAT IS LOVE?

Love is to feel deep affection for someone, a great interest and pleasure in something, love is to like or enjoy something very much.

All these things were expressed towards men after creation, because God delight greatly in men, he visited them every morning after creation.

Genesis 3:8

8 And they heard the voice of the Lord God walking in the garden in the cool of the day: and Adam and his wife hid themselves from the presence of the Lord God amongst the trees of the garden.

This visitation was confirmed in Psalm 8 when the angels questioned God about him visiting men regularly.

Psalm 8:4

4 What is man, that thou art mindful of him? and the son of man, that thou visitest him?

God did not express his love by visiting them only but after creation God bless men and gave men dominion over all his creation.

Genesis 1:28

28 And God blessed them, and God said unto them, Be fruitful, and multiply, and replenish the earth, and subdue it: and have dominion over the fish of the sea, and over the fowl of the air, and over every living thing that moveth upon the earth.

This was also confirmed by the Psalmist.

Psalm 8:5-8

5 For thou hast made him a little lower than the angels, and hast crowned him with glory and honour.

6 Thou madest him to have dominion over the works of thy hands; thou hast put all things under his feet:

7 All sheep and oxen, yea, and the beasts of the field;

8 The fowl of the air, and the fish of the sea, and whatsoever passeth through the paths of the seas.

DIFFERENT TYPES OF LOVE

There are different kinds of love but here I will discuss three basic loves.

EROS

This is the Greek word for erotic, this is physical love or sexual love between lovers, this love is often found between married couples (1 Corinthians 7:5), Hebrews 13:4). This love is mutual.

PHILOS

This is love between friends or families (Mathew 10:37 parents and children, John 11:3, 36 Yeshua and Lazarus, John 20:2 Yeshua and his disciples). This love is mutual also.

AGAPE

Agape love is the highest kind of love, it is the unconditional love of God towards mankind, as well as the human reciprocal love for God and towards our brethren.

John 3:16

16 For God so loved the world, that he gave his only begotten Son, that whosoever believeth in him should not perish, but have everlasting life.

This love was initiated by God and by Yeshua, and we were to follow suit.

Romans 5:8

8 But God commendeth his love toward us, in that, while we were yet sinners, Christ died for us.

The love started from God to Yeshua and from Yeshua to us and we must let the love flow through us to others.

John 15:9-13

9 As the Father hath loved me, so have I loved you: continue ye in my love.

10 If ye keep my commandments, ye shall abide in my love; even as I have kept my Father's commandments, and abide in his love.

11 These things have I spoken unto you, that my joy might remain in you, and that your joy might be full.

12 This is my commandment, That ye love one another, as I have loved you.

13 Greater love hath no man than this, that a man lay down his life for his friends.

GOD IS LOVE

God is not just loving but God himself is love.

1 John 4:7-8

7 Beloved, let us love one another: for love is of God; and every one that loveth is born of God, and knoweth God.

8 He that loveth not knoweth not God; for God is love.

WHEN LOVE IS LUST

Lust is a strong sexual desire towards someone, and it often confused with love, and it is the tool of Satan to pervert the world.

AGAPE (PERFECT) LOVE CAST OUT FEAR

Unlike other types of love that bring about fear and hatred, agape love cast out fear.

1 John 4:18

18 There is no fear in love; but perfect love casteth out fear: because fear hath torment.

He that feareth is not made perfect in love.

That is why we need to say always that God has not giving us the spirit of fear but of power, of love and of sound mind.

2 Timothy 1:7

7 For God hath not given us the spirit of fear; but of power, and of love, and of a sound mind.

Yeshua asked Peter three times, "Peter, do you love me?" to let it sink into him and the disciples that the love I am talking about is agape love and he later told him "feed my sheep".

John 21:15-17

15 So when they had dined, Jesus saith to Simon Peter, Simon, son of Jonas, lovest thou me more than these? He saith unto him, Yea, Lord; thou knowest that I love thee. He saith unto him, Feed my lambs.

16 He saith to him again the second time, Simon, son of Jonas, lovest thou me? He saith unto him, Yea, Lord; thou knowest that I love thee. He saith unto him, Feed my sheep.

17 He saith unto him the third time, Simon, son of Jonas, lovest thou me? Peter was grieved because he said unto him the third time, Lovest thou me? And he said unto him, Lord, thou knowest all things; thou knowest that I love thee. Jesus saith unto him, Feed my sheep.

POWER OF LOVE

Love is the strongest power on earth, it is the greatest commandment upon which all commandments hanged.

Matthew 22:36-40

36 Master, which is the great commandment in the law?

37 Jesus said unto him, Thou shalt love the Lord thy God with all thy heart, and with all thy soul, and with all thy mind.

38 This is the first and great commandment.

39 And the second is like unto it, Thou shalt love thy neighbour as thyself.

40 On these two commandments hang all the law and the prophets.

It was love that made God to give up Yeshua to this world, to save mankind.

John 3:16

16 For God so loved the world, that he gave his only begotten Son, that whosoever believeth in him should not perish, but have everlasting life.

The greatest of this unconditional love of God above speaking in tongues, above prophesy, above knowledge, above faith, and hope is explained in 1 Corinthians 13.

1 Corinthians 13

1 Though I speak with the tongues of men and of angels, and have not charity, I am become as sounding brass, or a tinkling cymbal.

2 And though I have the gift of prophecy, and understand all mysteries, and all knowledge; and though I have all faith, so that I could remove mountains, and have not charity, I am nothing.

3 And though I bestow all my goods to feed the poor, and though I give my body to be burned, and have not charity, it profiteth me nothing.

4 Charity suffereth long, and is kind; charity envieth not; charity vaunteth not itself, is not puffed up,

5 Doth not behave itself unseemly, seeketh not her own, is not easily provoked, thinketh no evil;

6 Rejoiceth not in iniquity, but rejoiceth in the truth;

7 Beareth all things, believeth all things, hopeth all things, endureth all things.

8 Charity never faileth: but whether there be prophecies, they shall fail; whether there be tongues, they shall cease; whether there be knowledge, it shall vanish away.

9 For we know in part, and we prophesy in part.

10 But when that which is perfect is come, then that which is in part shall be done away.

11 When I was a child, I spake as a child, I understood as a child, I thought as a child: but when I became a man, I put away childish things.

12 For now we see through a glass, darkly; but then face to face: now I know in part; but then shall I know even as also I am known.

13 And now abideth faith, hope, charity, these three; but the greatest of these is charity.

From verse 3 of this scripture, you will understand agape love better, giving to the needy is love but Paul says is not enough until it is Agape love and verses 4 to 8 now defines what agape love is.

It is the first of the fruit of the Holy Spirit.

Galatians 5:22-23

22 But the fruit of the Spirit is love, joy, peace, longsuffering, gentleness, goodness, faith,

23 Meekness, temperance: against such there is no law.

Agape love is hard to find, this is loving God above all other things and loving others as yourself.

Matthew 10:37

37 He that loveth father or mother more than me is not worthy of me: and he that loveth son or daughter more than me is not worthy of me.

BENEFITS OF LOVE

There are several benefits in loving God.

Love gives, God gave his best because of love.

John 3:16

16 For God so loved the world, that he gave his only begotten Son, that whosoever believeth in him should not perish, but have everlasting life.

When God loves you, he will give life for your life. Just as he has given his begotten for you he will give men for you also.

Isaiah 43:4

4 Since thou wast precious in my sight, thou hast been honourable, and I have loved thee: therefore will I give men for thee, and people for thy life.

All things will be working together for your good.

Romans 8:28

28 And we know that all things work together for good to them that love God, to them who are the called according to his purpose.

There is assurance of deliverance, lifting, answered prayer and more.

Psalm 91:14-16

14 Because he hath set his love upon me, therefore will I deliver him: I will set him on high, because he hath known my name.

15 He shall call upon me, and I will answer him: I will be with him in trouble; I will deliver him, and honour him.

16 With long life will I satisfy him, and shew him my salvation.

Preservation, the Lord preserve those that love him.

Psalm 145:20

20 The Lord preserveth all them that love him: but all the wicked will he destroy.

He is afflicted when we are afflicted, because of his love he feels our afflictions and he responded accordingly.

Isaiah 63:9

9 In all their affliction he was afflicted, and the angel of his presence saved them: in his love and in his pity he redeemed them; and he bare them, and carried them all the days of old.

Love changes curses to blessings.

Deuteronomy 23:3-5

3 An Ammonite or Moabite shall not enter into the congregation of the Lord; even to their tenth generation shall they not enter into the congregation of the Lord forever:

4 Because they met you not with bread and with water in the way, when ye came forth out of Egypt; and because they hired against thee Balaam the son of Beor of Pethor of Mesopotamia, to curse thee.

5 Nevertheless the Lord thy God would not hearken unto Balaam; but the Lord thy God turned the curse into a blessing unto thee, because the Lord thy God loved thee.

Chastisement, God correct those he loves through chastisement and that is a proof that you are his son or daughter.

Hebrews 12:6-7

6 For whom the Lord loveth he chasteneth, and scourgeth every son whom he receiveth.

7 If ye endure chastening, God dealeth with you as with sons; for what son is he whom the father chasteneth not?

HOW DO WE GET THE LOVE OF GOD?

Apart from the general love of God for mankind, there is a special love to those who believe in Yeshua and to get this love you must love God and you must love righteousness.

Psalm 11:7

7 For the righteous Lord loveth righteousness; his countenance doth behold the upright.

God love those who love him.

Proverbs 8:17

17 I love them that love me; and those that seek me early shall find me.

CHAPTER 2

GRACE

Grace is another attribute of God that is very unique, though grace of God does come to the righteous, but it is not about our good deeds, for grace is unmerited favor towards mankind and it a gift of God.

Ephesians 2:8-9

8 For by grace are ye saved through faith; and that not of yourselves: it is the gift of God:

9 Not of works, lest any man should boast.

As we can see grace is not of what we do but of God. None is deserved to live but God grace kept us.

Noah was the first person to obtain the grace of God. The whole world was corrupt, and God look down to destroy mankind, but Noah found grace with God just because God need someone to procreate mankind.

Genesis 6:1-8

1 And it came to pass, when men began to multiply on the face of the earth, and daughters were born unto them,

2 That the sons of God saw the daughters of men that they were fair; and they took them wives of all which they chose.

3 And the Lord said, My spirit shall not always strive with man, for that he also is flesh: yet his days shall be an hundred and twenty years.

4 There were giants in the earth in those days; and also after that, when the sons of God came in unto the daughters of men, and they bare children to them, the same became mighty men which were of old, men of renown.

5 And God saw that the wickedness of man was great in the earth, and that every imagination of the thoughts of his heart was only evil continually.

6 And it repented the Lord that he had made man on the earth, and it grieved him at his heart.

7 And the Lord said, I will destroy man whom I have created from the face of the earth; both man, and beast, and the creeping thing, and the fowls of the air; for it repenteth me that I have made them.

8 But Noah found grace in the eyes of the Lord.

There are 3 types of grace.

GENERAL GRACE

Refers to the blessings that God bestows on all of mankind regardless of their spiritual standing, this is rooted on the grace upon Noah.

Matthew 5:44-45

44 But I say unto you, Love your enemies, bless them that curse you, do good to them that hate you, and pray for them which despitefully use you, and persecute you;

45 That ye may be the children of your Father which is in heaven: for he maketh his sun to rise on the evil and on the good, and sendeth rain on the just and on the unjust.

Through this general grace the good were able to get to the next level of grace which is called saving grace.

SAVING GRACE

This grace is there regardless of the level of your sin he will take you in.

Ephesians 2:5

5 Even when we were dead in sins, hath quickened us together with Christ, (by grace ye are saved;)

All we need for saving grace to be activated in our life is to believe in Yeshua HaMashiach.

John 3:16

16 For God so loved the world, that he gave his only begotten Son, that whosoever believeth in him should not perish, but have everlasting life.

Regardless of whom you are just believe and call upon him you shall be saved.

Romans 10:11-13

11 For the scripture saith, Whosoever believeth on him shall not be ashamed.

12 For there is no difference between the Jew and the Greek: for the same Lord over all is rich unto all that call upon him.

13 For whosoever shall call upon the name of the Lord shall be saved.

And this know also that our ability to believe is also grace and a gift and if you are given to him he will not reject you.

John 6:37

37 All that the Father giveth me shall come to me; and him that cometh to me I will in no wise cast out.

After the fall of Adam, no man is longer qualified to be saved but through saving grace in Yeshua it was made possible.

Romans 3:10-12

10 As it is written, There is none righteous, no, not one:

11 There is none that understandeth, there is none that seeketh after God.

12 They are all gone out of the way, they are together become unprofitable; there is none that doeth good, no, not one.

Even the disciple of Yeshua doubted about their salvation and wonder who can be saved after Yeshua's comment about salvation, but Yeshua assures them that it is possible with grace.

Luke 18:25-27

25 For it is easier for a camel to go through a needle's eye, than for a rich man to enter into the kingdom of God.

26 And they that heard it said, Who then can be saved?

27 And he said, The things which are impossible with men are possible with God.

Men need to be thankful for the saving grace regularly, for it is not of what we do but of what Yeshua did by dying for us and it is a gift of God to us.

SUFFICIENT GRACE

It is also called grace for enablement. This grace operates only in the lives of a believers, this grace gives believers enablement to persevere in the presence of opposition, persecution, or afflictions. It changes your weakness to strength.

2 Corinthians 12:7-10

7 And lest I should be exalted above measure through the abundance of the revelations, there was given to me a thorn in the flesh, the messenger of Satan to buffet me, lest I should be exalted above measure.

8 For this thing I besought the Lord thrice, that it might depart from me.

9 And he said unto me, My grace is sufficient for thee: for my strength is made perfect in weakness. Most gladly therefore will I rather glory in my infirmities, that the power of Christ may rest upon me.

10 Therefore I take pleasure in infirmities, in reproaches, in necessities, in persecutions, in distresses for Christ's sake: for when I am weak, then am I strong.

This grace is very important and needed to be prayed for regularly and we need to be thankful always to God for this grace.

The enemy does everything imagined or unimagined but because of the grace of God we are not moved because we have received a kingdom that cannot be moved and because of this we should give grace to God.

Hebrews 12:28

28 Wherefore we receiving a kingdom which cannot be moved, let us have grace, whereby we may serve God acceptably with reverence and godly fear:

The general grace benediction that Paul shares at the end of his epistles are all sufficient grace for persecution of believers were rampant in those days.

2 Corinthians 13:14

14 The grace of the Lord Jesus Christ, and the love of God, and the communion of the Holy Ghost, be with you all. Amen.

Without this grace we can do nothing, without grace we cannot be alive, without grace we cannot be save, without grace we cannot stand.

If there is any time, we need sufficient grace it is now for the end is near and Satan has but a short time and now the systemic persecution of true believers is higher than ever.

GRACE CAN STOP WORKING

Unlike general grace saving grace and sufficient grace can be stopped in the life of a believers when we go back to sins.

Romans 6:1-2

1 What shall we say then? Shall we continue in sin, that grace may abound?

2 God forbid. How shall we, that are dead to sin, live any longer therein?

The worst still is if we desire to sin wilfully, for this is nailing Yeshua to the cross again, counting his blood unworthy and despising the spirit of grace and if there is no mercy we will not be restored.

Hebrews 10:26-29

26 For if we sin wilfully after that we have received the knowledge of the truth, there remaineth no more sacrifice for sins,

27 But a certain fearful looking for of judgment and fiery indignation, which shall devour the adversaries.

28 He that despised Moses' law died without mercy under two or three witnesses:

29 Of how much sorer punishment, suppose ye, shall he be thought worthy, who hath trodden under foot the Son of God, and hath counted the blood of the covenant, wherewith he was sanctified, an unholy thing, and hath done despite unto the Spirit of grace?

We need nothing to get the grace of God it is a gift, but only the genuine believers can obtain the sufficient grace of God.

CHAPTER 3

MERCY

WHAT IS MERCY?

Simply mercy is compassion or forgiveness shown toward someone whom it is within one's power to punish or harm.

Mercy in the kingdom of God is forgiveness or withholding punishment that is deserved.

We are all guilty of sin but God in his mercy sacrifice Yeshua HaMashiach on the cross to pay the price for our sins.

Mercy is that part of God that deals with judgement regarding our sins. It is the power of God to forgive and remove judgement and consequences of sins. Without the mercy of God, we will be consumed by either God or the devil.

Lamentations 3:22-23

22 It is of the Lord's mercies that we are not consumed, because his compassions fail not.

23 They are new every morning: great is thy faithfulness.

Mercy reverses judgement.

Mercy is, you are guilty of everything, you are to be punished, you are to be put to death, but I let you go.

The woman taken in adultery was guilty of death, but Mercy said go and sin no more, her deserved judgement was erased by mercy.

John 8:1-11

1 Jesus went unto the mount of Olives.

2 And early in the morning he came again into the temple, and all the people came unto him; and he sat down, and taught them.

3 And the scribes and Pharisees brought unto him a woman taken in adultery; and when they had set her in the midst,

4 They say unto him, Master, this woman was taken in adultery, in the very act.

5 Now Moses in the law commanded us, that such should be stoned: but what sayest thou?

6 This they said, tempting him, that they might have to accuse him. But Jesus stooped down, and with his finger wrote on the ground, as though he heard them not.

7 So when they continued asking him, he lifted up himself, and said unto them, He that is without sin among you, let him first cast a stone at her.

8 And again he stooped down, and wrote on the ground.

9 And they which heard it, being convicted by their own conscience, went out one by one, beginning at the eldest, even unto the last: and Jesus was left alone, and the woman standing in the midst.

10 When Jesus had lifted up himself, and saw none but the woman, he said unto her, Woman, where are those thine accusers? hath no man condemned thee?

11 She said, No man, Lord. And Jesus said unto her, Neither do I condemn thee: go, and sin no more.

Yeshua is the physical manifestation of mercy; his blood is the source of mercy and not just now but from the creation of this world.

PRODUCT OF LOVE AND GRACE

Mercy is a product of love and grace. The mercy of God operates in the area of judgement.

Bible says God is love.

1 John 4:8

8 He that loveth not knoweth not God; for God is love.

And through grace mankind was preserved through Noah's family.

Genesis 6:7-8

7 And the Lord said, I will destroy man whom I have created from the face of the earth; both man, and beast, and the creeping thing, and the fowls of the air; for it repenteth me that I have made them.

8 But Noah found grace in the eyes of the Lord.

But this is not enough to save mankind, for all have sinned and come short of the glory of God.

Romans 3:23

23 For all have sinned, and come short of the glory of God;

Thank God for mercy which came from love and grace of God, this was the blood of Yeshua that was shed at the foundation of this world.

The foundation of this world was laid on the blood of Yeshua and this is security for those who will believe on him.

Revelation 13:8

8 And all that dwell upon the earth shall worship him, whose names are not written in the book of life of the Lamb slain from the foundation of the world.

This blood that was slain for us from the beginning was made manifest at the cross to those who will believe.

1 Peter 1:18-20

18 Forasmuch as ye know that ye were not redeemed with corruptible things, as silver and gold, from your vain conversation received by tradition from your fathers;

19 But with the precious blood of Christ, as of a lamb without blemish and without spot:

20 Who verily was foreordained before the foundation of the world, but was manifest in these last times for you,

So, everything that the Lord was showing us from the beginning were a shadow of things to come including the law of Moses.

Hebrews 10:1

1 For the law having a shadow of good things to come, and not the very image of the things, can never with those sacrifices which they offered year by year continually make the comers thereunto perfect.

And this is where mercy comes in to avert the judgement of God and of the devil.

James 2:13

13 For he shall have judgment without mercy, that hath shewed no mercy; and mercy rejoiceth against judgment.

Mercy is all about judgement and whenever mercy comes against judgement mercy always comes out a winner.

Mercy of God overrides the judgement of God and of darkness in our life and vindicate us.

The mercy of God is as a result of the shedding blood of Yeshua.

Guilty or not guilty as long as you are born again and ask for mercy, the mercy in the blood of Yeshua justified you and save you from the wrath of God and men.

Romans 5:9

9 Much more then, being now justified by his blood, we shall be saved from wrath through him.

MERCY IS THE PLATFORM OF RECONCILIATION

Men are stiff-necked and disobedience and God could not relate with men anymore, but he could not because of the blood of Yeshua that was shed at the creation of the world and God for his love and compassion decided to come to us through the platform of mercy seat and in so doing men will not be consumed.

Exodus 25:21-22

21 And thou shalt put the mercy seat above upon the ark; and in the ark thou shalt put the testimony that I shall give thee.

22 And there I will meet with thee, and I will commune with thee from above the mercy seat, from between the two cherubims which are upon the ark of the testimony, of all things which I will give thee in commandment unto the children of Israel.

Atonement was made at the mercy seats and Yeshua became our atonement, today mercy seat is now the throne of grace and no matter what you are passing through and regardless of whom you are if you come to the throne of grace, you will obtain mercy.

Hebrews 4:14-16

14 Seeing then that we have a great high priest, that is passed into the heavens, Jesus the Son of God, let us hold fast our profession.

15 For we have not an high priest which cannot be touched with the feeling of our infirmities; but was in all points tempted like as we are, yet without sin.

16 Let us therefore come boldly unto the throne of grace, that we may obtain mercy, and find grace to help in time of need.

The Mercy Seat represented God in His dealings with sinful Israelites through the priest, and now Yeshua is that mercy seat through which God deals with sinful human race.

Romans 3:23-25

23 For all have sinned, and come short of the glory of God;

24 Being justified freely by his grace through the redemption that is in Christ Jesus:

25 Whom God hath set forth to be a propitiation through faith in his blood, to declare his righteousness for the remission of sins that are past, through the forbearance of God;

If the blood of animals can get mercy for the Israelites in the Old Testament, how much the blood of his precious son gets you mercy now.

Hebrews 9:13-14

13 For if the blood of bulls and of goats, and the ashes of an heifer sprinkling the unclean, sanctifieth to the purifying of the flesh:

14 How much more shall the blood of Christ, who through the eternal Spirit offered himself without spot to God, purge your conscience from dead works to serve the living God?

Now you can go to the throne of grace on your knee, in your prayer room, without any priest in barrier and you will definitely obtain mercy because Yeshua HaMashiach the great high priest has pave the way.

Are you under any judgement? Has your case been concluded? Was the verdict against you?

Mercy will change everything because mercy triumph over judgement.

James 2:13

13 For he shall have judgment without mercy, that hath shewed no mercy; and mercy rejoiceth against judgment.

No amount of judgment can handle mercy, for mercy endures forever and Satan cannot handle mercy for mercy is Yeshua HaMashiach.

MERCY DELIVERS WHEN ALL FAILS

We all need deliverance from the forces of darkness, and we all need to do one or several deliverance service in our life, but sometimes it seems all these didn't work.

When deliverance seems not to be working go to mercy. Where and when other forms of prayers seem not to be working mercy works.

One prayer that you really need when deliverance never come, after several attempts is the prayer of mercy. Even in crisis prayer of mercy work in place prayer of peace.

Sometimes you might not know the source of your problems or know fully well the history of your family or be able to remember or know where things went wrong. You might be a product of different nationality in a foreign land.

Your own problem might be from the womb, and no one tells you. You might be an adopted orphan that does not have a clue about your past. All you need is the prayers of mercy.

You might truly be guilty of all things; you might deserve death sentence. All you need is the prayers of mercy.

I am saying categorically today that you do not need to know all the source of your problems; you do not need to know all the history of your ancestors. All you need to know is mercy and Yeshua HaMashiach is mercy, he is the solution to all problems ask him for mercy for he is gracious and plentiful in mercy.

Exodus 34:6-7

6 And the Lord passed by before him, and proclaimed, The Lord, The Lord God, merciful and gracious, longsuffering, and abundant in goodness and truth,

7 Keeping mercy for thousands, forgiving iniquity and transgression and sin, and that will by no means clear the guilty; visiting the iniquity of the fathers upon the children, and upon the children's children, unto the third and to the fourth generation.

From verse 7 of the above scriptures God said I will forgive those who repent and will not spare those who refuse to repent. That is if you are willing and repent you will be forgive but if you refuse to repent you will be punished.

Isaiah 1:19-20

19 If ye be willing and obedient, ye shall eat the good of the land:

20 But if ye refuse and rebel, ye shall be devoured with the sword: for the mouth of the Lord hath spoken it.

Asking for mercy is accepting responsibility for all sins, both yours and your ancestors. There are several things we have done wrong in the past that we cannot remember, there are several wrongs we thought are rights.

Many of us have entered things we shouldn't have done either knowingly or unknowingly which is hunting us now. Our ancestors and parents have done things terrible that we cannot imagine, and the devil is taking advantage of all these to hold us down.

When you say Lord have mercy on me, you are saying indirectly Lord I am guilty and all I need is forgiveness and justice. And you will be justified.

Luke 18:13-14

13 And the publican, standing afar off, would not lift up so much as his eyes unto heaven, but smote upon his breast, saying, God be merciful to me a sinner.

14 I tell you, this man went down to his house justified rather than the other: for every one that exalteth himself shall be abased; and he that humbleth himself shall be exalted.

When Yeshua met blind Bartimaeus he did not bother to ask about his past because he asked for mercy, Yeshua assumed that he had already agreed he is guilty of all sins. So, all Yeshua could ask was "What wilt thou that I shall do unto thee?"

Mercy is too much to fail. Mercy never walks alone, his parents are grace and love, his companions are favor, truth, kindness, goodness, and his other names are compassion, forgiveness, grace, humanity, steadfast-love, lovingkindness and more.

Psalm 23:6

6 Surely goodness and mercy shall follow me all the days of my life: and I will dwell in the house of the Lord for ever.

Psalm 102:13

13 Thou shalt arise, and have mercy upon Zion: for the time to favour her, yea, the set time, is come.

MERCY AND GRACE

When you fall out of grace mercy could restore you if you genuinely repent and forsake your sins.

Mercy and grace are closely related, mercy is a product of grace and love.

God gave his son because he loves mankind.

John 3:16

16 For God so loved the world, that he gave his only begotten Son, that whosoever believeth in him should not perish, but have everlasting life.

And by the gift of grace yea re saved.

Ephesians 2:8-9

8 For by grace are ye saved through faith; and that not of yourselves: it is the gift of God:

9 Not of works, lest any man should boast.

Sometimes they are thought to be two sides of the same coin. Grace is a gift we don't deserve, while mercy is not getting the punishment we deserve.

Mercy is all about judgement and the punishment for sins. Mercy deals with deliverance from judgement and taking away of deserved punishments. We have all sin, and all deserve to die.

Mercy of God reverses any kind of judgement, afflictions, or punishments, either from God himself or the enemies.

Grace in other words is beyond judgement but include unmerited blessing, gifts, favor, and justice bestowed on mankind.

Grace is always there regardless of who you are if come to Yeshua you will be save.

Romans 10:12-13

12 For there is no difference between the Jew and the Greek: for the same Lord over all is rich unto all that call upon him.

13 For whosoever shall call upon the name of the Lord shall be saved.

Mercy unlike grace, though endures forever is not always there for everybody. Mercy is for believers that genuinely repented.

Grace of God is upon Esau, but the mercy of God is not upon him, simply because the Lord knows his ends from the beginning that he will not change.

Romans 9:13-16

13 As it is written, Jacob have I loved, but Esau have I hated.

14 What shall we say then? Is there unrighteousness with God? God forbid.

15 For he saith to Moses, I will have mercy on whom I will have mercy, and I will have compassion on whom I will have compassion.

16 So then it is not of him that willeth, nor of him that runneth, but of God that sheweth mercy.

That was why it requires sacrifices of blood every day in the Old Testament and now Yeshua has paid the price, but you need to be born again, pray and do the right thing to obtain mercy, particularly from the judgement of the enemies.

THREE TYPES OF MERCY

1 GOD GIVEN MERCY

This is not to everybody but for a few chosen men and women. David was a good example.

Romans 9:14-16

15 For he saith to Moses, I will have mercy on whom I will have mercy, and I will have compassion on whom I will have compassion.

16 So then it is not of him that willeth, nor of him that runneth, but of God that sheweth mercy.

2 MERCY YOU ASKED FOR

Prayer of mercy is very important, when you repent from your sins and pray earnestly for this mercy you will receive it. Even David upon all the mercies upon him never stops praying for mercy.

Blind Bartimaeus was not chosen for mercy, but he asked for it and get it.

Mark 10:47

47 And when he heard that it was Jesus of Nazareth, he began to cry out, and say, Jesus, thou son of David, have mercy on me.

If you are not a candidate of automatic mercy and you repent and asked God for mercy, you will get it but if you refuse to ask for it you will not get it.

Isaiah 1:19-20

19 If ye be willing and obedient, ye shall eat the good of the land:

20 But if ye refuse and rebel, ye shall be devoured with the sword: for the mouth of the Lord hath spoken it.

Even the condemned thief on the cross obtained mercy for he asked for it.

Luke 23:39-43

39 And one of the malefactors which were hanged railed on him, saying, If thou be Christ, save thyself and us.

40 But the other answering rebuked him, saying, Dost not thou fear God, seeing thou art in the same condemnation?

41 And we indeed justly; for we receive the due reward of our deeds: but this man hath done nothing amiss.

42 And he said unto Jesus, Lord, remember me when thou comest into thy kingdom.

43 And Jesus said unto him, Verily I say unto thee, Today shalt thou be with me in paradise.

3 MERCY, YOU GET BY SHOWING MERCY

Matthew 5:7

7 Blessed are the merciful: for they shall obtain mercy.

If you are merciful, you will receive mercy.

Psalm 18:25

25 With the merciful thou wilt shew thyself merciful; with an upright man thou wilt shew thyself upright;

And if you are not, you will not receive mercy.

James 2:13

13 For he shall have judgment without mercy, that hath shewed no mercy; and mercy rejoiceth against judgment.

NO SINNER WILL GO UNPURNISHED

Bible says no sinners can go unpunished which is very true.

Proverbs 11:21

21 Though hand join in hand, the wicked shall not be unpunished: but the seed of the righteous shall be delivered.

This is very true we will all reap what we sow but after giving our life our punishment will be for correction and when mercy comes it will reduce your period of punishment and put an end to it permanently.

We will all reap what we sow but the moment you stop sowing to the flesh and started sowing to the spirit shall reap life everlasting, though it may tarry do not give up for you will reap when mercy comes.

Galatians 6:7-9

7 Be not deceived; God is not mocked: for whatsoever a man soweth, that shall he also reap.

8 For he that soweth to his flesh shall of the flesh reap corruption; but he that soweth to the Spirit shall of the Spirit reap life everlasting.

9 And let us not be weary in well doing: for in due season we shall reap, if we faint not.

David was sinned and God gave him 3 option of punishment he chooses God punishment because he knew God will have mercy and God indeed show mercy and cut short the punishment.

1 Chronicles 21:7-17

7 And God was displeased with this thing; therefore he smote Israel.

8 And David said unto God, I have sinned greatly, because I have done this thing: but now, I beseech thee, do away the iniquity of thy servant; for I have done very foolishly.

9 And the Lord spake unto Gad, David's seer, saying,

10 Go and tell David, saying, Thus saith the Lord, I offer thee three things: choose thee one of them, that I may do it unto thee.

11 So Gad came to David, and said unto him, Thus saith the Lord, Choose thee

12 Either three years' famine; or three months to be destroyed before thy foes, while that the sword of thine enemies overtaketh thee; or else three days the sword of the Lord, even the pestilence, in the land, and the angel of the Lord destroying throughout all the coasts of Israel. Now therefore advise thyself what word I shall bring again to him that sent me.

13 And David said unto Gad, I am in a great strait: let me fall now into the hand of the Lord; for very great are his mercies: but let me not fall into the hand of man.

14 So the Lord sent pestilence upon Israel: and there fell of Israel seventy thousand men.

15 And God sent an angel unto Jerusalem to destroy it: and as he was destroying, the Lord beheld, and he repented him of the evil, and said to the angel that destroyed, It is enough, stay now thine hand. And the angel of the Lord stood by the threshingfloor of Ornan the Jebusite.

16 And David lifted up his eyes, and saw the angel of the Lord stand between the earth and the heaven, having a drawn sword in his hand stretched out over Jerusalem. Then David and the elders of Israel, who were clothed in sackcloth, fell upon their faces.

17 And David said unto God, Is it not I that commanded the people to be numbered? even I it is that have sinned and done evil indeed; but as for these sheep, what have they done? let thine hand, I pray thee, O Lord my God, be on me, and on my father's house; but not on thy people, that they should be plagued.

Though God get angry but because of mercy (favor) his anger will last but for a moment and soon you will be forgiven permanently.

Psalm 30:5

5 For his anger endureth but a moment; in his favour is life: weeping may endure for a night, but joy cometh in the morning.

The wage of sin is death, but the gift of mercy restores us and give us life eternal.

Romans 6:23

23 For the wages of sin is death; but the gift of God is eternal life through Jesus Christ our Lord.

But if you repent and still cannot stop sinning then the mercy will stop working just like grace.

Romans 6:1-2

1 What shall we say then? Shall we continue in sin, that grace may abound?

2 God forbid. How shall we, that are dead to sin, live any longer therein?

You must be a believer to get the mercy of God.

CHAPTER 4

FAVOR

WHAT IS FAVOR?

Favor is approval, support, or liking for someone or something or an act of kindness towards someone beyond what is due or usual.

Favor can also be defined as giving someone what they want or getting what you want from God or man.

But in the kingdom of God favor is about choice or preference. Favor of God is the aspect of God that deals with preferences of God, that is when God has to choose between two, you will be chosen.

This does not show that God did love others, but you will be the first in line for a miracle, this gives you advantage over others.

Favor gives you advantage or edge over all other gracious children of God, you will be best among equal. Whit favor when people are seated you will be standing and when people are standing you will be outstanding and when people are walking you will be running, and when people are running you will be flying.

Psalm 45:7

7 Thou lovest righteousness, and hatest wickedness: therefore God, thy God, hath anointed thee with the oil of gladness above thy fellows.

FAVOR AS PREFERENCE OR CHOICE

Before we continue let us get some good examples to explain favor as preference in the bible.

In the case of Esau and Jacob it is called love and hatred, God does not hate Esau as in human hatred, but it is favor for favor always prefers one to another.

Romans 9:12-15

12 It was said unto her, The elder shall serve the younger.

13 As it is written, Jacob have I loved, but Esau have I hated.

14 What shall we say then? Is there unrighteousness with God? God forbid.

15 For he saith to Moses, I will have mercy on whom I will have mercy, and I will have compassion on whom I will have compassion.

Esther was preferred among her competitors and was chosen. Bible said she obtain favor in the king sight more than all the virgins.

Esther 2:15-17

15 Now when the turn of Esther, the daughter of Abihail the uncle of Mordecai, who had taken her for his daughter, was come to go in unto the king, she required nothing but what Hegai the king's chamberlain, the keeper of the women, appointed. And Esther obtained favour in the sight of all them that looked upon her.

16 So Esther was taken unto king Ahasuerus into his house royal in the tenth month, which is the month Tebeth, in the seventh year of his reign.

17 And the king loved Esther above all the women, and she obtained grace and favour in his sight more than all the virgins; so that he set the royal crown upon her head, and made her queen instead of Vashti.

Mary the mother of Yeshua was said to be highly favored among women. She was not the best and only virgin in Israel at the time, but she was chosen because of favor.

Luke 1:28-30

28 And the angel came in unto her, and said, Hail, thou that art highly favoured, the Lord is with thee: blessed art thou among women.

29 And when she saw him, she was troubled at his saying, and cast in her mind what manner of salutation this should be.

30 And the angel said unto her, Fear not, Mary: for thou hast found favour with God.

It was favor of God upon Peter that made Yeshua to choose his boat for there were two ships in the lake.

Luke 5:1-3

1 And it came to pass, that, as the people pressed upon him to hear the word of God, he stood by the lake of Gennesaret,

2 And saw two ships standing by the lake: but the fishermen were gone out of them, and were washing their nets.

3 And he entered into one of the ships, which was Simon's, and prayed him that he would thrust out a little from the land. And he sat down, and taught the people out of the ship.

Getting married to a woman or man that truly fear God is God's favor for God choses for you.

Proverbs 18:22

22 Whoso findeth a wife findeth a good thing, and obtaineth favour of the Lord.

Israel was chosen among the nation of the world because Israel was favored.

Deuteronomy 7:6

6 For thou art an holy people unto the Lord thy God: the Lord thy God hath chosen thee to be a special people unto himself, above all people that are upon the face of the earth.

This is applied to believers all over the world today.

1 Peter 2:9

9 But ye are a chosen generation, a royal priesthood, an holy nation, a peculiar people; that ye should shew forth the praises of him who hath called you out of darkness into his marvellous light;

The word "For many are called but few are chosen" is talking about favor, that is among the called the chosen will be clothed with wedding garment.

Matthew 22:14

14 For many are called, but few are chosen.

FAVOR AS GETTING THINGS DONE

Favor is also getting what you want from God or man without delay, this favor is from God, and it extends to men too.

This was seen in the life of Samuel.

1 Samuel 2:26

26 And the child Samuel grew on, and was in favour both with the Lord, and also with men.

And in the life of our Lord Yeshua HaMashiach.

Luke 2:52

52 And Jesus increased in wisdom and stature, and in favour with God and man.

Regardless of whom you are dealing with believers or none-believers, they will give you what you want as long as you are his favorite, he makes even your enemy to favor you.

Proverbs 16:7

7 When a man's ways please the Lord, he maketh even his enemies to be at peace with him.

They might not like you, but they will help you because they cannot control the force of favor.

This favor was orchestrated by God in the life of the Israelites in Egypt.

Exodus 3:21

21 And I will give this people favour in the sight of the Egyptians: and it shall come to pass, that, when ye go, ye shall not go empty.

And by the time they were leaving Egypt they spoilt the Egyptians.

Exodus 12:36

36 And the Lord gave the people favour in the sight of the Egyptians, so that they lent unto them such things as they required. And they spoiled the Egyptians.

This kind of favor keep the eyes of the Lord, called his countenance upon you, and he will be getting things done for you by his angels or men wherever you go.

And this is how Israel were to be blessed according to Moses.

Numbers 6:23-27

23 Speak unto Aaron and unto his sons, saying, On this wise ye shall bless the children of Israel, saying unto them,

24 The Lord bless thee, and keep thee:

25 The Lord make his face shine upon thee, and be gracious unto thee:

26 The Lord lift up his countenance upon thee, and give thee peace.

27 And they shall put my name upon the children of Israel, and I will bless them.

Joseph was the best example of this favor; the eyes of the Lord was upon him everywhere he goes and Potiphar his master realizes this immediately and kept him in charge of everything.

Genesis 39:1-6

1 And Joseph was brought down to Egypt; and Potiphar, an officer of Pharaoh, captain of the guard, an Egyptian, bought him of the hands of the Ishmeelites, which had brought him down thither.

2 And the Lord was with Joseph, and he was a prosperous man; and he was in the house of his master the Egyptian.

3 And his master saw that the Lord was with him, and that the Lord made all that he did to prosper in his hand.

4 And Joseph found grace in his sight, and he served him: and he made him overseer over his house, and all that he had he put into his hand.

5 And it came to pass from the time that he had made him overseer in his house, and over all that he had, that the Lord blessed the Egyptian's house for Joseph's sake; and the blessing of the Lord was upon all that he had in the house, and in the field.

6 And he left all that he had in Joseph's hand; and he knew not ought he had, save the bread which he did eat. And Joseph was a goodly person, and well favoured.

Even in prison he was favored, and the prisoners were committed unto him.

Genesis 39:20-23

20 And Joseph's master took him, and put him into the prison, a place where the king's prisoners were bound: and he was there in the prison.

21 But the Lord was with Joseph, and shewed him mercy, and gave him favour in the sight of the keeper of the prison.

22 And the keeper of the prison committed to Joseph's hand all the prisoners that were in the prison; and whatsoever they did there, he was the doer of it.

23 The keeper of the prison looked not to any thing that was under his hand; because the Lord was with him, and that which he did, the Lord made it to prosper.

This favor got Joseph to the palace and the whole Egypt were committed unto his hand because the eye of the Lord is upon him.

Genesis 41:38-44

38 And Pharaoh said unto his servants, Can we find such a one as this is, a man in whom the Spirit of God is?

39 And Pharaoh said unto Joseph, Forasmuch as God hath shewed thee all this, there is none so discreet and wise as thou art:

40 Thou shalt be over my house, and according unto thy word shall all my people be ruled: only in the throne will I be greater than thou.

41 And Pharaoh said unto Joseph, See, I have set thee over all the land of Egypt.

42 And Pharaoh took off his ring from his hand, and put it upon Joseph's hand, and arrayed him in vestures of fine linen, and put a gold chain about his neck;

43 And he made him to ride in the second chariot which he had; and they cried before him, Bow the knee: and he made him ruler over all the land of Egypt.

44 And Pharaoh said unto Joseph, I am Pharaoh, and without thee shall no man lift up his hand or foot in all the land of Egypt.

FOUR TYPES OF FAVOR

1 GENERAL FAVOR

This is a common favor, and it can be upon several number of people for example all Israelites were favored by the Egyptian.

Exodus 3:21

21 And I will give this people favour in the sight of the Egyptians: and it shall come to pass, that, when ye go, ye shall not go empty.

And by the time they were leaving Egypt they spoilt the Egyptians because they were all favored.

Exodus 12:36

36 And the Lord gave the people favour in the sight of the Egyptians, so that they lent unto them such things as they required.

And they spoiled the Egyptians.

This favor is good, but it is not enough. All believers are in this level, level where we are sustained but God want us to sustain others so we must move to the next level of favored.

2 WELL FAVOR

This is having special advantage over others.

God give everyone something that makes us unique and when you are well-favored this uniqueness will be manifested, and you will excel.

This can be knowledge, skills, gifts, good looks, eloquent, or kindness.

This was the case of Leah and Rachel. Rachel was well favored because she was beautiful.

Genesis 29:17

17 Leah was tender eyed; but Rachel was beautiful and well favoured.

Esther was chosen among the virgins that were competing with her because well-favor gave her advantage over them.

Esther 2:15-17

15 Now when the turn of Esther, the daughter of Abihail the uncle of Mordecai, who had taken her for his daughter, was come to go in unto the king, she required nothing but what Hegai the king's chamberlain, the keeper of the women, appointed. And Esther obtained favour in the sight of all them that looked upon her.

16 So Esther was taken unto king Ahasuerus into his house royal in the tenth month, which is the month Tebeth, in the seventh year of his reign.

17 And the king loved Esther above all the women, and she obtained grace and favour in his sight more than all the virgins; so that he set the royal crown upon her head, and made her queen instead of Vashti.

Scientists are well favored, education is well favored, born rich is well favored, praying without ceasing is well favored.

Today witchcrafts and the wise men of this world are called well favored and advantageous over others because they believe they are wiser because of satanic knowledge, and they use this advantage to manipulate the world.

Nahum 3:1-4

1 Woe to the bloody city! it is all full of lies and robbery; the prey departeth not;

2 The noise of a whip, and the noise of the rattling of the wheels, and of the pransing horses, and of the jumping chariots.

3 The horseman lifteth up both the bright sword and the glittering spear: and there is a multitude of slain, and a great number of carcases; and there is none end of their corpses; they stumble upon their corpses:

4 Because of the multitude of the whoredoms of the wellfavoured harlot, the mistress of witchcrafts, that selleth nations through her whoredoms, and families through her witchcrafts.

The truth is that this knowledge is a fraction of the knowledge of heaven that Satan and his angel knew and gave to the so-called wise men of this world, but we the foolish believers are the well-favored for the foolishness of God is wiser than men.

1 Corinthians 1:25

25 Because the foolishness of God is wiser than men; and the weakness of God is stronger than men.

All being said well-favor is good but there is another level that is better and that is where God want us to be, and this level is called highly favor.

3 HIGHLY FAVOR

This is the peak of favor, this favor singles you out from among the well favored.

Bring out the best among equals, David was highly favored among his brethren and was anointed king even when his father never considered him.

Psalm 45:7

7 Thou lovest righteousness, and hatest wickedness: therefore God, thy God, hath anointed thee with the oil of gladness above thy fellows.

Mary the mother of Yeshua was highly favored. She was not the best and only virgin in Israel at the time, but she was chosen because she was highly favored.

Luke 1:28-30

28 And the angel came in unto her, and said, Hail, thou that art highly favoured, the Lord is with thee: blessed art thou among women.

29 And when she saw him, she was troubled at his saying, and cast in her mind what manner of salutation this should be.

30 And the angel said unto her, Fear not, Mary: for thou hast found favour with God.

Peter was highly favored, and his boat was chosen above the other.

Luke 5:1-3

1 And it came to pass, that, as the people pressed upon him to hear the word of God, he stood by the lake of Gennesaret,

2 And saw two ships standing by the lake: but the fishermen were gone out of them, and were washing their nets.

3 And he entered into one of the ships, which was Simon's, and prayed him that he would thrust out a little from the land. And he sat down, and taught the people out of the ship.

Though to be highly favored comes with high prices but when you get there you are unstoppable.

All great and good leaders are highly favored.

Moses was highly favored, Joshua was highly favored, David was highly favored, Yeshua was highly favored, Peter, Paul, and John the beloved were all highly favored.

Pray and confessed always to be highly favored.

Say I am highly favored in the name of Yeshua.

4 INCREASED FAVOR

Increased favor is a limitless favor that start from your level of favor. If you are at general level of favor, it will move you to well favored, if you are at well favored it will move you to highly favored and if you are at highly favored it will keep increasing.

Luke 2:52

52 And Jesus increased in wisdom and stature, and in favour with God and man.

As a believer in everything we must increase, Yeshua increase in wisdom, strength and favor, his mother was highly favored, but he did not stop there he increased from highly favored.

Increased favor is in on the class and level of its own, it is just saying and showing you are unstoppable.

You need to be born again to get the favor of God.

PRAYERS

Just like Peter's boat, your boat will be chosen among your peers and just like Mary you will be chosen among virgins just because you are highly favor.

Moses is chosen, Joshua is chosen, David is chosen, Yeshua is chosen, Peter, Paul, and John the beloved are all chosen you will be chosen in the name of Yeshua.

CHAPTER 5

WHICH IS THE GREATEST LOVE, GRACE, MERCY, AND FAVOR?

Love, grace, mercy, and favor of God are all great and they are all unique in operation, so you need the four to function well as a believer.

We all know that Love is God and God is the greatest.

1 Corinthians 13:13

13 And now abideth faith, hope, charity, these three; but the greatest of these is charity.

It all started with love, because of love God gave his best, his beloved son, himself which is his greatest possession.

John 3:16

16 For God so loved the world, that he gave his only begotten Son, that whosoever believeth in him should not perish, but have everlasting life.

And this begotten son is mercy of God.

Yeshua was trying to explain this to the Pharisees and the Sadducees that he is mercy when they were trying to tell him to avoid whom they called sinners.

Matthew 9:11-13

11 And when the Pharisees saw it, they said unto his disciples, Why eateth your Master with publicans and sinners?

12 But when Jesus heard that, he said unto them, They that be whole need not a physician, but they that are sick.

13 But go ye and learn what that meaneth, I will have mercy, and not sacrifice: for I am not come to call the righteous, but sinners to repentance.

This mercy is found in the blood of Yeshua, for without the shedding of blood there is no remission of sin.

Hebrews 9:22

22 And almost all things are by the law purged with blood; and without shedding of blood is no remission.

And if there is no remission of sin there is no forgiveness, if there is no remission of sin there is no grace.

Romans 6:1-2

1 What shall we say then? Shall we continue in sin, that grace may abound?

2 God forbid. How shall we, that are dead to sin, live any longer therein?

If there is no remission of sin, there is no favor.

Proverbs 28:13

13 He that covereth his sins shall not prosper: but whoso confesseth and forsaketh them shall have mercy.

MERCY IS THE GREATEST

Among love, grace, mercy and favor, mercy is the greatest because God choses it to be so, for through mercy you can find the others and not the other way round.

God is love, God is grace and mercy is the product of love and grace.

Yeshua is mercy and God gave all to his only begotten Son. He exalted mercy above love, above grace and above favor.

Philippians 2:9-11

9 Wherefore God also hath highly exalted him, and given him a name which is above every name:

10 That at the name of Jesus every knee should bow, of things in heaven, and things in earth, and things under the earth;

11 And that every tongue should confess that Jesus Christ is Lord, to the glory of God the Father.

Grace preserved mankind through Noah.

Genesis 6:7-8

7 And the Lord said, I will destroy man whom I have created from the face of the earth; both man, and beast, and the creeping thing, and the fowls of the air; for it repenteth me that I have made them.

8 But Noah found grace in the eyes of the Lord.

But grace does not remove the inherited sin from Adam, and all men were sinners through Adam and Eve.

Romans 5:12

12 Wherefore, as by one man sin entered into the world, and death by sin; and so death passed upon all men, for that all have sinned:

So, death reigns through mankind from Adam.

Romans 5:14

14 Nevertheless death reigned from Adam to Moses, even over them that had not sinned after the similitude of Adam's transgression, who is the figure of him that was to come.

Love and grace do not directly remove death but love and grace of God further give us a gift of salvation which is Yeshua HaMashiach which is mercy that remove death.

Romans 5:15

15 But not as the offence, so also is the free gift. For if through the offence of one many be dead, much more the grace of God, and the gift by grace, which is by one man, Jesus Christ, hath abounded unto many.

Mercy of God which is in the blood of Yeshua is what now remove the judgement and justified us.

Romans 5:16-19

16 And not as it was by one that sinned, so is the gift: for the judgment was by one to condemnation, but the free gift is of many offences unto justification.

17 For if by one man's offence death reigned by one; much more they which receive abundance of grace and of the gift of righteousness shall reign in life by one, Jesus Christ.)

18 Therefore as by the offence of one judgment came upon all men to condemnation; even so by the righteousness of one the free gift came upon all men unto justification of life.

19 For as by one man's disobedience many were made sinners, so by the obedience of one shall many be made righteous.

Mercy in the blood of Yeshua like I have told you is the aspect of God that deals with judgment, mercy is what justify you and save you from punishment of eternal death, wrong or right as long as you give your life to Yeshua genuinely you are justified.

Romans 5:9

9 Much more then, being now justified by his blood, we shall be saved from wrath through him.

And also, through mercy (Yeshua HaMashiach) we have eternal life.

John 3:16

16 For God so loved the world, that he gave his only begotten Son, that whosoever believeth in him should not perish, but have everlasting life.

Thus, mercy permanently remove death which is the wages or punishment for our sin and gives us eternal life.

In the Old Testament God could not relate with men directly because of sin and mercy became the platform through which God can relate with men, hence the mercy seat where atonement is made.

Exodus 25:21-22

21 And thou shalt put the mercy seat above upon the ark; and in the ark thou shalt put the testimony that I shall give thee.

22 And there I will meet with thee, and I will commune with thee from above the mercy seat, from between the two cherubims which are upon the ark of the testimony, of all things which I will give thee in commandment unto the children of Israel.

In the New Testament Yeshua (mercy) became our atonement, today mercy seat is now the throne of grace where we go directly to obtain mercy.

Hebrews 4:14-16

14 Seeing then that we have a great high priest, that is passed into the heavens, Jesus the Son of God, let us hold fast our profession.

15 For we have not an high priest which cannot be touched with the feeling of our infirmities; but was in all points tempted like as we are, yet without sin.

16 Let us therefore come boldly unto the throne of grace, that we may obtain mercy, and find grace to help in time of need.

MERCY NEVER WALK ALONE

Among the four love, grace, mercy and favor, mercy never walk alone.

In Psalm 23:6 he was with goodness.

Psalm 23:6

6 Surely goodness and mercy shall follow me all the days of my life: and I will dwell in the house of the Lord forever.

When mercy comes, favor immediately follows.

Psalm 102:13

13 Thou shalt arise, and have mercy upon Zion: for the time to favour her, yea, the set time, is come.

When you obtain mercy, you will immediately find your lost grace.

Hebrews 4:16

16 Let us therefore come boldly unto the throne of grace, that we may obtain mercy, and find grace to help in time of need.

The day mercy was to walk alone she still met with truth.

Psalm 85:10

10 Mercy and truth are met together; righteousness and peace have kissed each other.

When mercy come salvation come.

Psalm 119:41

41 Let thy mercies come also unto me, O Lord, even thy salvation, according to thy word.

You can get all other three from mercy and not the other way round. When you fell out of love mercy can bring you back.

Daniel 9:9

9 To the Lord our God belong mercies and forgivenesses, though we have rebelled against him;

Micah 7:18-19

18 Who is a God like unto thee, that pardoneth iniquity, and passeth by the transgression of the remnant of his heritage? he retaineth not his anger for ever, because he delighteth in mercy.

19 He will turn again, he will have compassion upon us; he will subdue our iniquities; and thou wilt cast all their sins into the depths of the sea.

When you fell out of grace mercy can restore you.

Hebrews 4:16

16 Let us therefore come boldly unto the throne of grace, that we may obtain mercy, and find grace to help in time of need.

When you fell out favor mercy can bring it back.

Psalm 102:13

13 Thou shalt arise, and have mercy upon Zion: for the time to favour her, yea, the set time, is come.

Several places in the bible uses love, grace, and favor of God in place of mercy of God.

Twice God has decided not to talk to men anymore, but mercy brought him back. Just as God endure forever so his mercy endures forever.

Psalm 136:1-3

1 O give thanks unto the Lord; for he is good: for his mercy endureth for ever.

2 O give thanks unto the God of gods: for his mercy endureth for ever.

3 O give thanks to the Lord of lords: for his mercy endureth for ever.

Yeshua is mercy and God has highly exalted him and given him a name above others for his glory.

Philippians 2:9-11

9 Wherefore God also hath highly exalted him, and given him a name which is above every name:

10 That at the name of Jesus every knee should bow, of things in heaven, and things in earth, and things under the earth;

11 And that every tongue should confess that Jesus Christ is Lord, to the glory of God the Father.

MERCY CAN DO IT

Mercy can do all what the four can do, but love, grace, and favor work through mercy to do most things.

Mercy is love, mercy is grace and mercy is favor because you can find them all through mercy, mercy is the greatest.

CONCLUSION

With love, grace, mercy, and favor of God upon your life you are already a god unto you enemies.

Exodus 7:1

1 And the Lord said unto Moses, See, I have made thee a god to Pharaoh: and Aaron thy brother shall be thy prophet.

Those things you cannot do before will become so easy. For the fullness of these four make all things possible for you.

Matthew 19:26

26 But Jesus beheld them, and said unto them, With men this is impossible; but with God all things are possible.

When love, grace, mercy, and favor of God is operating fully in your life, they automatically add the power and authority of God unto you for they subdue and hinders the power of Satan and his agents operating against you.

At this stage power of resurrection and life, power of restoration, power to pursue, to overtake and power to recover all will be working in your life like never before.

For with love all things work together for your good, with grace you can continue against all odds, with mercy you are victorious and with favor you prosper.

APPENDIX PRAYERS

I receive the love, the grace, mercy, and the favor of God in the name of Yeshua.

I receive grace to sustain the love, the grace, mercy, and the favor of God in the name of Yeshua.

I love the Lord and all things are working together for my good in the name of Yeshua.

I am a product of grace I am unstoppable in the name of Yeshua.

PERSONAL DELIVERANCE PRAYERS.

Scripture Confession:

Confess the following deliverance scriptures, you can add your own relevance scriptures.

Isaiah 49:24-26

24 Shall the prey be taken from the mighty, or the lawful captive delivered?

25 But thus saith the Lord, Even the captives of the mighty shall be taken away, and the prey of the terrible shall be delivered: for I will contend with him that contendeth with thee, and I will save thy children.

26 And I will feed them that oppress thee with their own flesh; and they shall be drunken with their own blood, as with sweet wine: and all flesh shall know that I the Lord am thy Saviour and thy Redeemer, the mighty One of Jacob.

2 Timothy 4:18

18 And the Lord shall deliver me from every evil work, and will preserve me unto his heavenly kingdom: to whom be glory for ever and ever. Amen.

Galatians 3:13-14

13 Christ hath redeemed us from the curse of the law, being made a curse for us: for it is written, Cursed is every one that hangeth on a tree:

14 That the blessing of Abraham might come on the Gentiles through Yeshua Christ; that we might receive the promise of the Spirit through faith.

Galatians 5:1

1 Stand fast therefore in the liberty wherewith Christ hath made us free, and be not entangled again with the yoke of bondage.

PRAISE & WORSHIP (5-10 minutes)

Use any relevant praise and worship song to saturate you and your environment.

Prayer:

Father, I thank you for this moment of deliverance, I thank you for you will never fail me, I thank you for sustaining me till this moment. I cover this environment with the blood of Yeshua.

I cover my spirit, soul and body, my mind, will and emotion, my senses, my bodily organ and element, my bodily system, my aura and energy system with the blood of Yeshua.

I ask Holy Spirit to take absolute control of everything in the name of Yeshua.

I take authority over satanic atmospheres created by cultic activity, destiny altering images, incantations, ill spoken words, witchcrafts in the name of Yeshua.

I take authority and I change this atmosphere to godly atmosphere; I command the spiritual climate to shift, physical climate to shift and I say let there be light in the name of Yeshua.

I command that this atmosphere must be filled with the Glory of God. Father fills the atmosphere, fills the environment with Your Glory.

I alter this environment and declare it is now suitable for my prayers to thrive, the will of God to thrive and I establish a supernatural environment for deliverance to occur in the name of Yeshua.

STEP ONE

1 Confession and repentance

1 John 1:9

9 If we confess our sins, he is faithful and just to forgive us our sins, and to cleanse us from all unrighteousness.

Leviticus 26:40-42

40 If they shall confess their iniquity, and the iniquity of their fathers, with their trespass which they trespassed against me, and that also they have walked contrary unto me;

41 And that I also have walked contrary unto them, and have brought them into the land of their enemies; if then their uncircumcised hearts be humbled, and they then accept of the punishment of their iniquity:

42 Then will I remember my covenant with Jacob, and also my covenant with Isaac, and also my covenant with Abraham will I remember; and I will remember the land.

I Confess and repent of my sins, sins of my parents, sins of my generation, and the sins of my ancestors in the name of Yeshua.

I repent of the sins of idolatry, Witchcrafts, hatred, murder, abortion, cheating, stealing, adultery, fornication, uncleanness, drunkenness, child molestation, incense, oppression, sodomy, raveling, pride, lie, falsification, and other sins I have committed knowingly or unknowingly in the name of Yeshua.

Father in your mercy withdraw every legal ground of Satan and his agents have to attack me in the name of Yeshua.

2 Genuinely forgive those who offended you.

Mark 11:25

25 And when ye stand praying, forgive, if ye have ought against any: that your Father also which is in heaven may forgive you your trespasses.

Father in the name of Yeshua I forgive everyone that have sin against me in one way or the other. I live them in your hand in the name of Yeshua.

STEP TWO

Break all covenants:

Zechariah 9:11

11 As for thee also, by the blood of thy covenant I have sent forth thy prisoners out of the pit wherein is no water.

There are lots of covenants to break ranging from ancestral, blood to cosmic energy, they are different with individuals. This is just a pattern. As God keep opening your eyes, you keep breaking them.

Prayers:

I break and lose myself from every evil covenant operating in my life in the name of Yeshua.

I break and lose myself from every evil covenant I enter into knowingly or unknowingly in the name of Yeshua.

I break and lose myself from every evil covenant enter into by anyone on my behalf knowingly or unknowingly in the name of Yeshua.

Also, remember to break the covenant of your enemies too, they have covenant with Satan, with death and hell and they have that protect them. Break them.

Isaiah 28:18

18 And your covenant with death shall be disannulled, and your agreement with hell shall not stand; when the overflowing scourge shall pass through, then ye shall be trodden down by it.

Prayers:

I break covenant backing up my enemies in the name of Yeshua.

I break all covenant backing up the battle I am fighting in the name of Yeshua.

(Get the prayer book on breaking all curses and covenant)

Break all curses:

Galatians 3:13-14

13 Christ hath redeemed us from the curse of the law, being made a curse for us: for it is written, Cursed is every one that hangeth on a tree:

14 That the blessing of Abraham might come on the Gentiles through Yeshua Christ; that we might receive the promise of the Spirit through faith.

Just like covenant there are several curses to break too. Ranging from Biblical curses, ancestral, foundational, generation to personal curses. Different with individual.

Curses and covenant are what give demons legal ground to operate in our lives. They are the spirit behind every covenant and curses.

(Get the prayer book on breaking all curses and covenant)

Prayers:

I break and redeem my life from personal curses, parental curses, generational curses, foundational curses, and ancestral curses in the name of Yeshua.

I break and redeem my life from any curses operating in my life by the blood of Yeshua in the name of Yeshua.

STEP THREE

Claim your blessings.

Galatians 3:14

14 That the blessing of Abraham might come on the Gentiles through Yeshua Christ; that we might receive the promise of the Spirit through faith.

Prayers:

I declare and decree that I am blessed in the name of Yeshua.

I am blessed and it cannot be reverse in the name of Yeshua.

I claim the blessing of Abraham, I claim all lost generational blessings all the way to Adam and Eve in the name of Yeshua.

STEP FOUR

Pull down altars.

Altars is the authentic spiritual portals, gate or access to the spiritual realm, it is a place where divine and human world meet.

Effective evil sacrifices and rituals are done at the altars, information, and instructions to demons against believers are carried out from the altars.

Altars opens your and closes your spiritual doors. There are several altars to be destroyed in our lives.

(Get the prayer book on breaking all curses and covenant)

Prayers:

I raise an altar with blood of Yeshua, and I pull down every altar raise against me in the heaven, on earth, in the water, in my father's house, in my mother's house, in my place of birth, in my environment, in my place of work in the name of Yeshua.

Every priest making sacrifices against me in any altar, fall down and die with the altar in the name of Yeshua.

Blood of Yeshua cancel every blood sacrifice speaking against me in the name Yeshua.

STEP FIVE

Renunciation:

Father in the name of Yeshua I renounce, break and loose myself from all forms of witchcrafts, familiar spirits, marine spirits, spirit spouses, ancestral spirits, all occults, death and hell, evil dedication, and initiations in the name of Yeshua.

I renounce, break and loose myself from all other religions, especially Roman Catholicism, Hinduism, Islam, Idolatry, Christianity, and other religions in the name of Yeshua.

I renounce, break and loose myself from all demonic subjection to any man or woman spirits living or dead, birds' spirits, animal spirits, reptilian spirits, animate or inanimate objects in the name of Yeshua.

I renounce pride, rebellion, disobedience, stubbornness, and self-centeredness. I also renounce unbelief, doubt, lies, fear, hatred, and anger in the name of Yeshua.

STEP SIX

Break soul ties and soul contracts.

There are many soul ties to break write then down as you remember and break them.

Father, I break and renounce all evil and ungodly soul ties that I have ever had with forces of darkness (witchcrafts, ex-sexual partners, associates, and other forms of religions) in the name of Yeshua. I cancel any soul contracts ever form with any entities past present and future in the name of Yeshua.

STEP SEVEN

Saturate yourself again in the blood of Yeshua by saying:

I soak my Spirit, soul, and body in the blood of Yeshua seven times.

Lay your hand on your head and the other hand on your belly button and pray like this:

Holy Ghost fire burn from the top of my head to the sole of my feet. Begin to mention every organ of your body by saying: Holy Ghost Fire burn on every organ of my body.

Repeat this seven times:

I drink the blood of Yeshua; I swallow the fire of the Holy Ghost.

STEP EIGHT

Bind and cast out related spirits.

Matthew 18:18

18 Verily I say unto you, Whatsoever ye shall bind on earth shall be bound in heaven: and whatsoever ye shall loose on earth shall be loosed in heaven.

Mark 16:17

17 And these signs shall follow them that believe; In my name shall they cast out devils; they shall speak with new tongues;

Through the blood of Yeshua, I am redeemed out of the hand of the devil and all my sins are forgiven. I hold the blood of Yeshua against you Satan. I belong to Yeshua now spirit, soul, and body.

Satan has no more power over me, no more place inside of me. I renounce all evil spirits completely and declare them to be my enemies.

I bind strong demons, prince of the power of the air, principalities, powers, rulers of darkness of this world and spiritual wickedness in high places in the name of Yeshua.

I bind spirit of death and hell, I bind witchcrafts, marine spirits, familiar spirits, elemental spirits, serpentine spirits, reptilian spirits, Beelzebub, birds and animal spirits in the name of Yeshua.

Yeshua said: "And these signs shall follow them that believe: In my name shall they cast out devils: ...." (Mark 16:17).

I am a believer, and in the name of Yeshua HaMashiach, I exercise my authority and expel all evil spirits. I command them to leave, according to the Word of God and in the name of Yeshua. Amen.

I ask for legions upon legions of angels from heaven in the name of Yeshua to war on my behalf in the name of Yeshua.

Father in heaven, please send your Holy Spirit to fill me up in the name of Yeshua.

Keep quiet: then take a deep breath and breathe out (repeat about 7 times).

STEP NINE

Ask again for the Holy Spirit to fill you anew and afresh.

Seal yourself with the blood of Yeshua and with the fire of the Holy Ghost.

Breath in and exhale and breath in and exhale again as you are saying I breathe in the blood of Yeshua; I breathe in the fire of the Holy Ghost as long as you wish.

Close with praise and worship songs

Remember deliverance is a process. To fully attain your deliverance and possess your possession you must do this several times, days, months, and years. We are to pray without ceasing.

m justified by the mercy of God, and I am saved from every wrath in the name of Yeshua.

I am highly favored so my enemies who claimed to be well favored cannot take advantage of me in the name of Yeshua.

REFERENCES:

Unless otherwise noted, all Scripture quotations are from the King James Version of the Bible.

https://languages.oup.com/google-dictionary-en/

About the Author

ABOUT THE AUTHOR: Joshua Olumoye is the founder and Pastor of Harmony Heavenly Church a fellowship of genuine believers of Yeshua HaMashiach. He authored more than twenty books, including *For his glory, Far superior host, Far superior weapons,* and the best-selling books *Russia and China leads in end time.* With the ability to rightly dividing the word through grace of God, he easily brings out the truth of the mystery of the bible.

After The Storm

Allandria Dawson

BookLeaf
Publishing

India | USA | UK

Presentation by *BookLeaf Publishing*

Web: www.bookleafpub.com

E-mail: info@bookleafpub.com

ISBN: 9789358314717

First edition 2024

First of the Month

Who put you in a box?
Someone else or yourself?
There's an infinity of firsts
At your fingertips
Go
Enjoy
Explore
You are the writer
You own the pen
And when you're feeling stuck
Let today be a reminder
Of the million other things you can try
The light is green
It's time to choose
Win or win?

W _ R

Hug your people
Pick up the phone
Express your love
Make amends
Whatever you must do to rest peacefully
Get it done
While you have the chance
This world is ruled by uncertainty
Don't let a second go to waste
Time is unforgiving

Art

There's something about being drawn...
Whether it be on
Or in
Consider a canvas
Decorated with pastel strokes of navy and jade
Capture every soft edge
Every sharp line
Ombré like the shades of my love
Textured like the skin on my hand
To be drawn in a strangers image

Consider the tide
Forever faithful to a cyclical demise
But beautiful every.single.time

No art supplies needed
I'm designing with my mind
Seeking past what my eyes can provide
I'm drawn

To question my existence
Find love then do something different
Be better than what's expected
Drawn to the next exit
Of life

So Far Gone

Lost in her eyes
I drank the poison this time
There's something about the way she smiles
At me like she can read my mind
They warned me about you
But I had to give it a try

Transition

At some point I shed my skin
Outgrew my old self
And craved a change
It took me years to leave
Courage isn't cheap

Can I ask you something?

How many pictures did you take before you
found the perfect one
How many duplicates are in your photo album
as waste
When I saw you I knew
It was always you
I wonder why you don't believe
That you are a 10/10
Made in his image

I am human

I get coffee sometimes just to hold it
As symbol of productivity
When self expectations are low
And the only thing I could do was sit up in bed
I remember to get a coffee
If not on the bad days
Which i have often
Definitely on the good
Because it's ok to grab a coffee
It's ok if that's all i did today

Acid

I roam the halls tracing where your fingers last
touched
Smell the clothes that your body laid in
It's true that you never ask me for much
except for admission into my museum

The historic paintings of moments passed
And pain etched into stone
And of course the blank canvases that cradle the
room

To allow space for growth
You stare and want to know more
I'll help as much as I can
But I don't know when the museum will close

Matrimony

I don't want a title or control
I want what's beyond a piece of paper
What transcends a ceremony
And lingers throughout time

I want your soul to crave mine
The way our ancestors fought for freedom
Strongly, urgently
With thoughts of the future in their back pocket

I want to break barriers with you
And become the best version of ourselves
Create the life we deserve
And give back to the world

I want everything that is YOU
Not to be possessive though
But to have the privilege to experience and
admire you for the rest of my life
So even though I don't care about the paper
I'm going to make you my wife

Find It

Your light
Some energy
The strength
To do
Be
Exist
Live
And thrive
Get up
I SAID GET UP
Fuck your old ways
I know you're tired
You must find IT

Honestly, truly

Is it bad that the whole time I was on the plane I
kept hoping it'd crash
Because that'd be less painful than going back to
you

Once upon a time

Some people won't experience love
So I guess I'm blessed
To love the same girl twice
Within one life
I'll never grow tired of seeing her smile
Caressing her skin
Or watching her win
Her victories are mine
We share everything
But we shine on our own
Two beautiful beings
I love her the way that a Gardner tends to their fields
Continuously with compassion
Making up for what's lacking
I crave her body and her mind
She's my fix every time
Rooted in me
Oh so fine
The love of my life

Winter

And then I realized
I was wrestling with a breeze
The only way to win
Was to surrender

Moon

And when the sun sets
I do not desire goodnights
But promises of see you later
And
Talk to you tomorrows
Because this love knows no end
You cannot just close the book of us at night

My White Flag

Will you take me into the library of your mind
So, I can trace my fingertips across the pages of
your thoughts
We can file away the remnants of us
Will you just sit with me for a while?
Pull me close like you used to
And tell me about your day?
It's the little things
With every synchronized breath I'm affirming
myself
What's mine will find its way to me
And with every tear
I'm reminded that we are both working towards
our dreams
And though it's painful
I'm squeezing into a space in your life
That I know I'm too big for
I call a truce

Lottery

Angel numbers hitting
But my angel is missing
Damn

Dear Younger Self

There's so many places I wanted to take you
Where the world meets the edge
And the water is turquoise
And the mountains are high
And the air smells sweetly
Where our troubles died
Where we can feel alive
It's so beautiful there

Destination

Could it be?
The softest place I've ever been
So fluffy that the clouds greeted me with envy
Sun kissed
Resting in my peace
Heart and mind open
As I breathe
I receive
My lungs expand with air so crisp
It's intoxicating
Take another hit

You can't bottle this
It's almost indescribable
The view surpasses surreal
Seeing colors that I'm certain are not of this
world
Unearthly
Time was just numbers

To be savored by sight
And digested with a sweet "mmm"
My soul sat next to me that day
And we received rest

Could it be?
Have I arrived?

The Truth

I am more than fun and humor
more than dollars and cents
I am not calm and cool
I'm a mountain of emotions
A hot mess if you will

Realization

21

I think the greatest way that I can show my love
for you
Is to let you go

Me @ Me

I decided to love you
Reshape how you receive and how you give
And show you that there's more to life than this
Than bodies
Than feelings
Than materialistic things
Go to the earth
And just breathe
Just be with me

From your toes
To your shoulders
To your crown
And when you feel overwhelmed
You can say this sound

You are great
You are magical
You are strong
You are powerful
You make a difference
People love you
You are really loved
You have purpose
You are safe

You are kind
You are successful
Your needs are met
You are changing
You're like a butterfly
And it's so beautiful

www.ingramcontent.com/pod-product-compliance
Lightning Source LLC
Chambersburg PA
CBHW071253140726
47996CB00007B/2839